CRUSH DEPTH

CRUSH DEPTH

MICHAEL SPENCE

Truman State University Press
New Odyssey Series

Published by Truman State University Press, Kirksville, Missouri USA
tsup.truman.edu
© 2009 Michael Spence
New Odyssey Series
All rights reserved

Cover image: *Descent*, by Dan Spence. Used by permission.

Cover design: Teresa Wheeler
Type: Minion Pro © Adobe Systems Inc. and Myriad Pro © Adobe Systems Inc.
Printed by: Edwards Brothers, Ann Arbor, Michigan USA

Library of Congress Cataloging-in-Publication Data

Spence, Michael, 1952 Feb. 21–
Crush depth / Michael Spence.
    p. cm. — (New odyssey series)
ISBN 978-1-931112-90-1 (pbk. : alk. paper)
1. United States. Navy—Officers—Poetry. 2. Fathers and sons—Poetry. I.
Title.
PS3569.P4455C78 2009
811'.54—dc22

                                                                    2009009850

The paper in this publication meets or exceeds the minimum requirements of
the American National Standard for Information Sciences—Permanence of
Paper for Printed Library Materials, ANSI Z39.48–1992.

for my father,
James W. Spence
(1922–1993)

CONTENTS

III. THE UNBROKEN CODE

ACKNOWLEDGMENTS

Grateful acknowledgment is made to the following publications in which some of these poems first appeared:

The American Scholar: "Darken Ship," "The Right Way to Escape from a Sinking Ship," and "Roundabout"

The Amicus Journal: "The Fig Curtain of Atherton"

The Antioch Review: "An Engineering Problem"

Barrow Street: "The Safety Officer's Account: Letter, Report, Journal"

The Chariton Review: "Class Portrait"

The New Criterion: "The *Darter* and the *Dace,* the Way I Wish He'd Told It"

The New Republic: "Addendum to the Safety Officer's Account"

Nimrod: "My Father Washing Dishes (I)" and "My Father Washing Dishes (II)"

The North American Review: "Father Gathers His Breath" and "The Unbroken Code"

Poetry: "Saudade" © 1996 by the Modern Poetry Association

Poetry Northwest: "The Bayou Drive-In"

Press: "Anchored Out" and "Nisqually Bay"

The Seattle Review: "The Little Penguins of Prince Phillip Island"

The Sewanee Review: "Below Decks" and "Palawan Passage" (first published in vol. XX, no. 1, Spring 1991, and vol. 115, no. 4, Winter 2007, respectively)

Southwest Review: "Oracle"

Tar River Poetry: "A Southern Vintage: Mount Aitken Winery, South Australia, 1986"

"The Right Way to Escape from a Sinking Ship" is reprinted from *The Spine* (Purdue University Press, 1987)

"The Safety Officer's Account: Letter, Report, Journal" was
    reprinted in *Pontoon #8: An Anthology of Washington State
    Poets* (Floating Bridge Press, 2005)
"Oracle" was reprinted on the *Verse Daily* website (May 16, 2006)
"Darken Ship" and "Roundabout" were reprinted in *Limbs of
    the Pine, Peaks of the Range: Poems by Twenty-Six Pacific
    Northwest Poets* (Rose Alley Press, 2007)

For their advice on my work, my thanks and deep gratitude to
John Davis, Susan Landgraf, Judy Lightfoot, Robert McNamara,
Sati Mookerjee, Arlene Naganawa, Judith Skillman, and Ann
Spiers; to the Sewanee Writers' Conference; and especially to my
wife, Sharon Hashimoto, whose constant support and inspiration
helped me to assemble the past.

I. DARKEN SHIP

SAUDADE

—"the desire to be afar"

A boy, I moved from coast to coast,
Learning that five years was as long
As a home in any state could last:
To stay in one place for good was wrong.

The Portuguese explorers knew
This hunger—the urge that makes a man
Seek another world. The blue
That lined their west pulled the sun

Beyond their shores. The sailors wondered
Where the sun kept going. What country
Could call down such fire like a bird
To a branch, fusing sky and sea?

A man, I feared the fog and rain
Of Seattle would seal me in their gauze.
So I joined the poster navy: men
Turned gold by the sun, like all those

Who search for home in the horizon.
Five years I crossed the Atlantic
Until my own land had grown foreign:
Strange enough to call me back.

BELOW DECKS

Three chevrons on his shoulder like the Vs
Of victory proclaimed this bosun mate
Was first class. BM1 Heckenmueller—
Fat, red-haired, mostly drunk—was Falstaff
Built squat. Our ship looping the center
Of the Mediterranean, for two bucks a head
He'd roll a double feature from the scores
Of reels packed in his locker. *No charge
For you,* he'd tell me; *you own the theater.*

Lying cramped as a warren underneath
The port quarter—a sponson where the crew
Came to heave the ship's trash into the sea—
My office would fill first with sailors, then
With smoke, as if instantly smoldering
From their desire. When the room went dark,
How right it was that the screen we raised
Was the sheet off a bed.

                              The flick that night
Begins like most: opening shot of a bed flat
As the ocean, and cue the man and woman stripped
Of sound and color—words for the private act
Made flesh. He mounts her, and the sailors
Cry the low moans and yells while the couple
Couples. A few moments, then she's on top.

That's when I see the two are professional
Wrestlers—the captain of the tag team,
The man breaks the hold of passion by patting

Her hip, and their positions change: now
She's down on all fours, he behind her; now
They're both head to crotch.

                            The second surprise
For me: she is truly beautiful—voluptuous body,
Sculpted face, and the spark missing from women
In most of these films. When I see her face
Laugh, I believe she really enjoys making love;
And I think how lucky the man is, I think
How I'd spend hours touching her, ignoring
The director's call to move certain ways
For the camera, his scream of *Cut!* Just
As I picture the woman walking off the set
With me, the film stops—the white glare
Of plain light on the sheet.

                            Though officers
And crew alike laughed behind his back, today
I know why we needed, even feared, Heckenmueller:
His body molded in the sweet grip of the lusts
Rubbing us. When I looked close, I could see—
As if caught behind his eyes—the small image
Of myself.

RECRUITERS

1. 1974: SEATTLE STATION

America, it seems, is not at war
This year. But the lieutenant lets me
Hoist my hand, a flag of flesh—the navy
No longer has the draft which blew in scores
Of those just like me, afraid to crawl
In jungle shadows. The hot air of pride
Filling my chest like a sail, I take the course
Laid out: a line of stitches through the squall
Of OCS to a floating airport that slides
Above the seas, too big to notice their force.

2. 1978: CAPTAIN'S MAST

Like fingers in his pocket, the five joints
Became a hand the Shore Patrol had caught—
They grabbed and shook it hard. I see the pot
Arranged like dried-out rifle shells: they point
At my sailor. The captain chuckles, *Stokes is in big
Doobie doo-doo.* He faces the man: *The best part
Of you ran down your mother's leg.* His hitch
Is ending, I object. *Stokes gets the brig,*
The captain grins ... *or he re-ups.* My chart
Now blotched and frayed, I feel the vessel's pitch.

ANCHORED OUT

They call them Campfire Girls. I turned to stare
At the women Oscar nodded toward. They wore
Miniskirts and see-through blouses, their arms
Crossed over their breasts, trying to stay warm
Around a giant stack of burning tires.
The smoke roiled up, fingering their hair,
Making them squint. They drew close to the flames
And waved at us. This didn't fit the dreams
I'd had of foreign romance. Crossing water
That seemed to quarantine us from the shore,
We had hit the beach to take our liberties
In Naples. We passed by velvet tapestries
Of Elvis, Christ, and sneering bullfighters
That spread out like tongues from the trunks of cars.
I stopped when Oscar said, *There's Humpty-Dumpty!*
Her mouth slightly open, her gaze empty,
A woman fat and wrinkled sat on a wall
Beyond the hey-joes' wares. *They say she's still
At work,* said Oscar; *the oldest whore around!*
Of course I had to laugh. But a squeaky sound
Escaped my throat, and she looked right at me.
Instead of cursing, she smiled. I felt my knees
Wobble, my skin prickle—her eyes were blue
As Donna's, the first girl I ever knew.
My fingers tingled to stroke her face. *What's wrong?*
Said Oscar. *Let's get a drink.* Before long,
We sat in a smoky bar, listening to rock
And drinking fire. When we stumbled to the dock,
Lights on the pier, as in a fairy tale,

Made the water at our feet gleam like marble.
I watched it shimmer as the groaning boat
Took us back to the ship: a castle in a moat.

THE LANDLOCKED SEA

The aircraft carrier looms too large
To damage. With its jets, we rule
The seas. The officer in charge
Of the Basic Point Defense Missiles

(Which my men call BEEpiDEEmus),
I think of a Greek god—shorter
Than the rest, he can merely toss
Pebbles while the others hurl spears

Of lightning. One dawn in the dark cavern
Of Combat Central, I'm told: *Get your launchers
Manned up—the cruiser off our stern
Is Russian, and its firing radar*

*Is locked on us. Where are the jets?
They're all on deck. When do they go up?
That might make the Russian shoot.
The captain says you're it.* The blip

On the scope—smaller than a speck—
Glows green as seaweed. I lean
On a wall of dials. If the cruiser strikes,
They won't record the light bursting in.

CLASS PORTRAIT

The ship required a simple photograph:
A shot of all its petty officers
Who'd re-enlisted during the first half
Of the Med cruise. My boss said: *Ensure*

Your sailor, BM2 Rousseau, shows up
Tomorrow with the rest on the flight deck.
I explained the guy was off the ship
On leave and wouldn't be back for a week.

My boss frowned, then smiled. *Well, Gordon's yours,*
Isn't he? And he's a second-class.
Tell him he's standing in for Rousseau. The chore
Seemed easy enough. But Gordon shouted: *My ass!*

I'm getting the hell out of this goddamn nav
In six months—you think I want my face
With all those fools who re-upped? I ain't no slave,
And I'll be damned if I take Rousseau's place

Just 'cuz him and me are black. We stood
On the fantail, watching the ocean melt
The sun: the brine we sailed on was an acid
That ate even the light itself. I felt

So stupid—why hadn't I seen how wrong
The whole thing was? I returned to tell my boss
Gordon refused and that I went along
With him. The commander sighed: *That's his loss—*

This isn't a request. Inform him if
He won't comply, I'll put him in the brig.
I said that Gordon didn't deserve such grief—
He was the best one on the fueling rig

And never got in trouble. *Do your job,*
Ensign, the commander ordered. Gordon cursed
When he heard—*Guess I'm just another slab*
Of dark meat. At OCS, I'd rehearsed

Giving orders like these, but that was play.
I said I'd make it up to him; this was not
My doing. A good man, he went the next day
To the flight deck. The sailors in the shot

Are formed into a large 67,
The ship's hull number: like a graduation shot
From some high school. You can't tell if the men—
Shrunk to dots by distance—are black or white.

ORACLE

"If a charlatan makes a hundred predictions and
chance brings about the fulfillment of one of
these, the others are forgotten and the one remains
as a token of God's favor and as proof of a miracle."
—Voltaire, *The Age of Louis XIV*

I have called for a fleet of ships
To go down—explosions, hulls
Splitting, all hands lost—
To reach the one that sinks.
In distant countries I see dictators
Fall like rotten fruit: a colonel
In his limousine is blown up.
Every tea leaf shows me
An Armageddon. When those who doubt
Confront me, I say the future is
Hazy. My crystal ball may fog
When I try to read which movie star
Will marry what millionaire,
Which candidate gets elected
Or shot. Entrails, tarot cards,
Star charts, computers: the tools
Change; my trade does not. No matter
What their vision, people come to me.
I search the strings of accidents
They believe in. With the common thread
Drawn loose by magic, I weave them lives.

THE SAFETY OFFICER'S ACCOUNT:
LETTER, REPORT, JOURNAL

I must inform you with regret your son,
Seaman David Holt, was killed at sea.

> *While taking on a load of diesel fuel*
> *From the oiler, USS* Columbia,

>> We looked like a construction crew—hard hats
>> And life vests—but we weren't building anything.

Liked by the whole crew, your son performed
His duties well—you can be very proud

> *Our ship rolled sharply to port as the oiler*
> *Heeled to starboard, just before the nozzle*

>> I'd turned my eyes away: I thought I'd seen
>> A dolphin in the roil between the vessels.

Of how he served his country. His tragic death
Is a great loss for the Navy. My condolences—

> *Of the fueling rig was securely seated.*
> *The spanwire snapped: SN Holt was cut in half.*

>> How often had I told him not to stand
>> So close to the pad-eye? The noise, a gunshot

And those of the whole service—go out
To you. Your son's belongings will be sent

> *Though medics responded quickly, the sailor died*
> *On the fueling station. Despite warnings*

>> In a steel room, made every one of us
>> On the sponson crouch or dive to the deck.

To your address when they've been inventoried.
Arrangements to return your son's remains

> *From BM1 LeBlanc and myself, Holt*
> *Was standing aft of JP Riser Two*

>> At first I didn't know that Holt was hurt:
>> Then feared he'd been knocked overboard.

Are now in progress; please contact me
As to the disposition you desire, or if

> *When the spanwire parted. Responsibility*
> *For this accident is mine. I wish to note*

>> I mistook his blood for diesel fuel
>> Pooling in the shade behind the riser.

You have any questions at any time.
On behalf of the entire fleet,

> *That BM1 LeBlanc should not be cited*
> *With any negligence, if such a charge*

>> The sailors looked away from each other,
>> And from me. I clutched the bulkhead, stared—

I send to you my deepest sympathies
On the loss of your son David. I remain ...

> *Is subsequently raised. I've taken care*
> *Of notifying kin. Respectfully,*

>> Now the waves looked less like fins.
>> I don't believe the dolphin was ever there.

ADDENDUM TO THE SAFETY OFFICER'S ACCOUNT

           When the spanwire
Snapped like a line mooring Seaman Holt
To this world, the severing released a flood
Of paper from his body, and I had to fill
Every sheet with words.
                 A month washed by—
I'd written the letter to his family,
The accident report, the memoranda
To the various departments that had fed
And clothed and paid him, my journal entry—
His face began to lose its puzzled look,
Dissolving in the darkness of my thoughts.

The Shore Patrol had fished him out of bars,
Disorderly and drunk; he'd been written up
For ragged dungarees, skipping watch
On the quarterdeck and unrep duties
On fueling details. His final day, though,
He was on that rig.
            Then Personnel
Called for a Terminal Evaluation.
In every category on the form—
Skills, discipline, personal appearance—
I wrote a 4.0. The yeoman typed
From this a "smooth eval" which I proofread.
The comma at the end I whited out
To a period.

TRUE

George bowed his head and shut his eyes
To the shot of the naked woman slid
By Lieutenant Jaech between the slides
Of weapons systems—Tomahawk
And Phoenix missiles, ASROCs—"to keep
You brand-new ensigns awake." Surprised
At first by glowing flesh amid
The finned and rigid pipes of death—
As though a nun who played the organ
At Mass had kissed him—George dropped his gaze
(And focused on Claire, his fiancée
In Iowa) till he heard the click
Of another slide. But his classmates
At Surface Warfare School betrayed him
To the "Lewd-tenant." Jaech then laid
Like mines three shots back to back: girls
Who kneeled with hands behind their heads
(The way of captured prisoners,
George realized). Before his eyes
Could close, their light burst in on him.

Aboard the aircraft carrier,
Assigned to Deck Department, George—
The ensign "green as seaweed," joked
His fellow junior officers—
Would write Claire letters promising
That he'd stay true: *I'll save myself
For the honeymoon.* He steered past bars
Whose siren jukeboxes would pound

His bosun mates till they filled themselves
With beer as if to contain a sea
The way the Med for sleepless weeks
Had held them captive. In Capri,
While his peers pursued the girls who browned
In string bikinis on glinting sand
(The waves like tongues that licked the beach),
George volunteered to help some locals
And caught a bus at dawn each day
Into the hills to paint a church.
His arm grew numb whitewashing walls
Until his liberty was gone.

After seven months of blasting jets
From the flight deck ("the ship getting
Its rockets off," guffawed his peers),
Of oilers pumping diesel fuel
Through hoses huge and black ("here comes
Moby's dick," his sailors laughed)
The carrier released its anchor
Off the shores of Malaga.
To celebrate their going home,
His bosun mates invited George
To join them for a "victory toast."
He wanted to refuse, but his pulse
Sped up—excitement? fear?—
When they insisted: "Come on, sir!
How often do you survive the Med?"
The boat ride over loosened him

A little. Country western songs
Entwined with smoke inside the place
They took him to. Sangria, sweet
And sharp as oranges, woke his tongue.

He sang the tunes he'd sung with Claire
Back home, with men—*his* men!—who'd spent
So long imprisoned out at sea.
In Spain with Johnny Cash! he marveled.
The woman sitting next to him:
Where had she come from? She grinned
Wider than Claire each time he sang
Or spoke about his life on the ship.
She rubbed his leg. He laughed and drank
Until the bar began to turn
(Like that carousel in Iowa,
George thought), to turn into a room
Whose bed he lay down on with her
Between him and the cool, blue sheets.
I want to marry you, he groaned
As lightning seared his skin. The click
Of flashbulbs made him jerk. His men
Wagged cameras, laughing. Into her hair—
So dry it crackled at his touch—
He lowered his head and closed his eyes.

DARKEN SHIP

At night, to keep the enemy
From spotting us, our lights dimmed red:
An ember's color which at sea
Won't travel far. My recruiter had said

The camaraderie of the sailors
And sights I'd see would give me tales
For home. But on my carrier—
A ship huge as a glacier of steel—

Who could even meet the whole crew?
To watch the stars, I'd step out
On the port quarter: the place we threw
Our garbage overboard. That night,

As I lounged in a far corner,
Someone backed onto the ledge.
I need more time! he cried. Two other
Shadows pushed him to the edge.

I yelled—two shapes stiffened to ice,
The third halfway over the rail.
The red lights, smudging each face,
Made comrades of us all.

THE RIGHT WAY TO ESCAPE
FROM A SINKING SHIP

It may start with a torpedo or missile,
A tracer striking the magazine, making
A deadly gift of light. Between wars,
Your enemies will be reefs, icebergs,
Other ships sunk just below the surface.

So many things can show you how thin
Your hull always was. You won't believe
How fast the water rushes in, trying
To cleanse you for all the time you've ridden
Its back. When your metal world starts

To list, climb the tilting ladder quick:
You must be on deck for the sea's muster
Before it fills the hold—your final cargo.
Remember to flee the lower side: pretend
You are scaling a mountain of steel

That grows steeper every moment. Make sure
No debris, like your shipmates, is floating
Below you. Heed the chaplain: cross yourself.
Cross your arms over your chest; cross
Your ankles to guard your crotch. Then jump

Like a spear—straight, with a small splash.
The ocean rewards the fancy diver
With a blackout or broken limbs. Its surface
May be fire. Flaming oil is good cover
When you're shot at. Swim underwater

As far as you can. Trick your lungs: pretend
You are breathing by sucking in your stomach.
Paddling your hands back and forth beneath
Your burning ceiling, you can make a hole
For a short gasp. When you rise beyond it,

And you see the ship going down, the time
For flight is gone. Lie on your back: pretend
You are boneless as a jellyfish. Water
Funneling down stacks into the boilers
May blow your ship to shrapnel—turning

Even that refuge into thousands of knives.
Put a hand between your legs or the blast
Will impale you. When the sea at last seems
Calm again, look for boats, survivors: pretend
There are some and they are looking for you.

If you see none, swim for whatever floats—
To survive you must find something to cling to.
And if there is not a single kapok jacket
Or stick of wood, one last thing may save you.
Relax—take a breath, and bow your head

Into the water. Some have lived hours, lifting up
Only for air. Stay calm; keep your mind blank.
Let the sea hold you, feel your face: pretend
When it knows you, you can fool it: pretend
You are already dead.

II. SHELLBACK

A SNAPSHOT OF MY FATHER
FROM THE WAR
—Australia, 1942

You stand on Brisbane's beach—the sand flames
Around your feet—with two buddies whose names

Vanished like so much else since the "Good Fight."
And you grin, rendered in the black and white

That war became. The waves of your dark hair
Catch sunlight like the surf rolling fire to shore.

The crackerjacks you wear—against the regs—
Are tailored; sharp and tight around your legs,

They draw the sheilas' flirty looks. Cap set back
On the crown of your head (another black

Mark if caught), you absorb this lazy scene
For the stint when the tunnel of your submarine

Encircles your body. You face the afternoon sun:
In the deep dark, you'll meet the Rising One.

THE LITTLE PENGUINS
OF PRINCE PHILLIP ISLAND
—Australia, 1986

What I expected was a crowd as small
And quiet as the penguins'. But here, people
Multiply the darker it gets—they fill
The concrete benches with their babble
As if at a drag race in the States. *When will*
They get here? whine some kids. I think of the trail
Back home I hiked with my sister: four miles
Up steep switchback to Deer Lake. The air was full
Of radios; wrappers and beer bottles
Crowded the shore like the people who came all
That way to stay the same. A loudspeaker tells
Us that noise and bright lights can startle
The birds, so please, no flashbulbs or yells
From the audience. Then, out of the swell
Of the surf glides the first—like the waves that roll
In, it merges black with white. And I recall
Their other name is *fairy.* More of the them sail
Ashore, shake themselves and begin, their goal
The burrows in the dunes behind us. Up the aisles
Between our rows of seats they have to waddle,
Separated as if from wild animals
By a painted line and steel handrails.
Before they can get close, flashbulbs dazzle
Them, and a camera crew with portable
Klieg lights swoops down. Some of the birds huddle
Together; a few run back. But soon, the little

Penguins start coming again. They file
Past us, not looking our way at all,
Seeing only one light, hearing only one call.

THE FIG CURTAIN OF ATHERTON
—Queensland, Australia

In a land named
For a queen, life kneels only
To older royalties. The eucalyptus—
Bark in shreds
As if flayed by the wind—
Pulls a kookaburra out of the sky.
The bird drops
The seed of a fig tree
Among the top branches. Sending roots
Thin as vines
Down the trunk, the seed
Erects a stalk. Before the fig can reach
Soil or sky,
Something—wind, disease,
A sudden shift of the earth—fells the tree
Against another.
The fig keeps growing roots: a fibrous curtain
That will not part.
Generations of sloths
And koalas climb the ropes of wood.
At last the leaning
Eucalyptus dies,
Rotting away. In the world, what reigns
Is what survives.
The wind, with majesty,
Flows through it, trying to make a harp
Of this gnarled rib cage.

A CAIRNS IDYLL

Oblivious to starfish chewing up
The coral of the Great Barrier Reef,
While Dad walks off for tickets for our trip

To watch its vanishing, I lounge and leaf
Through Chaucer as a palm tree pricks my back.
The fronds clack overhead—tongues gone stiff

With salt and sun. I can't keep track
Of where the story leads, trying to ignore
The sea beyond me. Medieval spellings frac-

Ture my attention, and my eyes grow sore
From footnotes. I try to raise lust for the wench
Of Bath while waves pull sparks of light ashore.

A *thump!* I feel through my buttocks makes me flinch:
The coconut rocks to a stop. I shift to a bench.

A SOUTHERN VINTAGE: MOUNT AITKEN
VINEYARD, SOUTH AUSTRALIA, 1986

Following an arrow and a whim,
We found a building on a hill: it lay
Like an animal bludgeoned by the heat.
I squinted as we crossed the dusty lot.
The door snapped to behind, blinding us—
Dark and cool as the inside of a cask.
A sun-creased man, leaning against the shelves
Of bottles which glowed as though filled with genies,
Straightened for his only customers.

My father said *Guh-die.* The barman frowned,
Standing stiffer than the hairs of his crew cut.
Yanks on holiday? he asked. Dad nodded,
Seeming not to hear the scornful tone.
Embarrassed for my father, I felt exposed
By this country where the roads and seasons ran
Opposite to what I knew. Dad went on:
*Yes, sir; my first time here, my holiday
Was the working kind—aboard a submarine.*

The man stared, then slapped his hands on the bar:
You're the blokes who saved us from the Japs!
He grinned. *Hang on a tic.* He disappeared
Behind a curtain that shimmered like the heat outside,
Returning with a bottle. *This is the stuff
The first G.I. knew drank with me
On V-J Day.* The wine poured black as port.
He clunked his glass against my father's, nodding:
Here's to you, mate, and all your fellow heroes.

My dad a hero? A man whose hair, once black
With waves, now lay becalmed to a flat gray;
A man stooped slightly forward as if prepared
To shy away from any kind of touch.
I tasted something bitter in the wine
Filling the glass I held; it pricked my tongue,
The insides of my mouth. I couldn't talk
About the things my father kept as deep
As men inside a sub, the things he said

To a barkeeper he'd never seen before.
Holding my tumbler up to the dim light
I saw the liquid, an ocean small and dark,
Edge the rim with red: a trace of blood
From sailors claimed by distant seas. Shrugging,
My father smiled: *We did our duty.* To cork
That ghost of sun and grit, I brought a bottle
Home—as though believing I could join
Some ship it might have held.

THE *DARTER* AND THE *DACE*, THE WAY I WISH HE'D TOLD IT

The Darter *refused to sink,* my father said
Almost to himself, gluing together
The toy submarine I'd sent away for.
I looked at him; he kept his gaze on the pieces.
We were out on patrol, the two of us,
Up off the northeast coast of Australia.
Guess what we find? I shook my head, leaning
Closer—he'd never spoken of the war.
The main fleet of the Japanese Navy.

He dabbed at some glue with a cloth. *That shocks*
Us and *the bad guys; we've been searching*
For that fleet a long while. In my mind
An ocean glinted: metal wedges spiked
With guns. I asked what happened. *We both fire*
Our torpedoes, then scramble out of there.
At least we try to. All those ships coming
After us, and you know what? The Darter,
Our sister boat, runs aground.

The sound of iron scraping over reefs
Raised goose bumps down my back. Dad blew
On a seam to make it dry. *Of course my sub,*
The Dace, *has to turn around and rescue*
The stranded crew. The enemy's getting nearer
As we get the guys aboard. But we can't leave yet.
I asked why not. *Secrets,* he said;
A submarine is packed with secrets. We need
To take a ton of records off that boat.

I said that that must be when the *Dace* escaped.
Attaching the conning tower, Dad grimaced:
Nope. You know what's a sub's biggest secret?
He tilted the vessel slightly. *The sub itself.*
We can't let the Darter *be captured intact,*
So we have to sink it. We start with this:
He tapped the plastic deck gun with his finger.
But that just raises little puffs of dust
Here and here and here, he poked the hull.

He tapped it some more, a sort of Morse code,
Then turned the toy till the bow pointed at me.
So we shoot torpedoes at it. I saw
The blurry white of their contrails streak away.
Grinning, I said those "fish" blew up the *Darter.*
We see some plumes of water and think that, too.
But when the mist clears, damn sub's still there.
The enemy destroyers are nearly here.
He spun the toy's propeller. *Time to leave.*

So *that* was when the *Darter* got captured, I said,
Imagining a boarding party sloshing
Like acid through its metal corridors,
Dissolving the secret stuff that Dad had known.
His square of sandpaper rubbed and smoothed
The back fins. *Not exactly. The Japs send*
A plane in low and drop a bomb on it.
He gave a shrug that left his eyebrows raised.
You could say the enemy does our job for us.

I nodded, said it was too bad the *Darter*
Got all blown up. My father blew away
The fine grit his sanding had scoured loose.
Mmm-hmm, except the Zero pilot's aim
Is a bit shy. The blast bangs up the sub
Without destroying it. Lifting the toy
To the kitchen light, Dad shut one green eye
And sighted along its length. *A tough sewer pipe.*
He looked at me. *You know what finally happens?*

His breath eased in and out. *The war ends,*
We go home, the years sail by—but the Darter
Stays stuck on that reef. With a smile brief
As a splash, he held the sub out to me.
Now kids play on it, jumping into the sea.
I carefully took the boat. When he placed his hand
On my shoulder, I saw explosions of water:
I saw those children climb the torn hull,
Laughing and calling inside the empty dark.

PALAWAN PASSAGE
—for James W. Spence,
Radio Technician First Class

I.

Inside the sub—a crowded narrow tunnel
Half-blocked by hatches and ladders; the air
A faint haze of oil and sweat—he takes
His post: the radio shack, a cramped niche.
To be the vessel's ears is his assignment,
To separate the noise of enemies
From every other oceanic sound.

The Army Air Corps washed him out: He was told
Pressure changes in the rising altitudes
Would injure his ears. So he joined the Navy,
Which sends him to the only kind of craft
(He shakes his head) designed to sink.

Ordered to report to the USS *Dace*,
He looks the sub's name up: "A type
Of carp." Why not *Shark?* he wonders.
Or *Piranha?* Only after he's come aboard
Will the bosun tell him: *Carp'll eat
Every other fish in a pond—to kill 'em,
You gotta drain the goddamn pond.*
A short burst of laughter escapes his lips
Like air released from far down underwater.

Beneath his feet (unsteady as his nerves),
The deck lurches like a seesaw when the sub
Dives. He feels pressure push against his ears—

The way, as a kid, he'd press his thumbs in them
When he didn't want to hear.

    II.

To him it's just an accident the day
The *Dace,* patrolling Palawan Passage
With only its sister boat the *Darter,*
Rounds a headland and finds the Rising Sun
Whipping from the masts of an entire fleet:
The Japanese Center Force,
Steaming hard for Leyte Gulf.

Every Allied vessel has been searching
For the armada his sub has stumbled on.
The two of them fire their torpedoes
Which in no time slam the flagship *Atago,*
Sinking it. The enemy swerves toward them.

In their race to retreat, the *Darter*
Runs aground on Bombay Shoal.
His sub must turn around to save those sailors.
Soon as they're aboard, the *Dace* plummets
And barely ducks a swooping plane.

Sort of fun, he grins—like a roller coaster.
That's when the thought hits him: he could drown.
What would his obituary say?
If he survives, he'll tell his son this story.

He's mulling what words he'll use when pinging
Loudly rings his ears. Four great blasts
Convulse the sub. Diving steeply to escape,
It rams the bottom. He's thrown sideways, bangs
His head on a shelf. The yells of sailors reach him,
And other sounds he's never imagined: rasping
Of hull across reefs; hollow booms
As it pounds the ocean floor. Yanking himself
Back into his seat, he's sure the racket will bring
More destroyers: how could they not hear this?

As if trying to twist it apart, the current scrapes
And bashes the sub, dragging it for miles.
Then the *Dace* is released—the boat has been swept
Beyond the depth charges and all pursuit.

Down to mushroom soup and peanut butter,
With barely enough fuel to get back
On one engine, the *Dace* returns to port.

For all the battering, little damage
Is visible. Gouges are patched, dents
Hammered out. Seeing the boat from dockside,
He's stunned to hear he's part of history:
People are calling Leyte Gulf the greatest
Naval battle of modern times. His ears
Still ring—a pitch too high to name—as the sub
Immerses him in the dark haunts he must listen to.

THE DESERT PINNACLES

I.

The columns of rock stand
Upright like men. The wind,
Crossing an ocean to shrill
Their edges, makes them crumble,
As though angry with
Whatever blocks its path.
North and south, this coast
Is parched: the only forest
That can endure is one
Whose trees are made of stone.
The wind scours these trunks
Ceaselessly, and shrinks
Their knobby forms a grain
Of sand at a time. The dunes
Grow, scattering a tide
Of glitter like seeds.

II.

Before this land was land,
Before a hot wind
Ever touched these stones,
This country was ocean.
For millennia the shells
Of dead crustaceans fell
In spirals through dark water,
Burying the floor.
Gradually, the sea fell
After them, falling till

The sky reached the ground.
Up through the shells that crowned
The drying mud, a forest
Of cypress grew—masts
Of a sunken fleet. The woods
Finally died and rotted.
Centuries of rain
Dissolved the shells. Down
The liquid sank, lime
Mixing with it. In time
Its minerals coated the roots
Like underground stalactites.
Blowing the sand away,
The wind slowly displayed
The columns—they marked like tombstones
Each place a tree had grown.

III.

Epochs had wavered passed
When ships of the Dutch East
India Company sailed
In view of these pillars. *An old
City in ruins*, thought the sailors—
They would not come ashore.

IIII.

Hissing, the wind fills
My lungs like empty sails.
As I walk across the plain—

Its sand orange as the sun—
I feel some urge to kick
The small plugs of rock
That crunch under my soles.
Cemented to the soil,
When kicked they skitter away,
Tinkling like pottery.
Then I regret trying to force
Music from them. Fierce
As a gale, the wind consumes
Their notes, rasping its claim
That it will conquer all.
The roots the Pinnacles
Started from are dust:
*Now the columns will just
Wear away,* I believe.

IIIII.

I learn I'm wrong—they gave
The land a shape it will keep
For eons. As the minerals seep
Deeper, the shells continue
To descend, adding new
Layers to the cores
Of stone, building towers
Underneath the sand:
Teeth to bite the wind.

WAKING LATE

Come see the sunrise, son!
I groaned, rolling over
Slow as a sodden log
The waves attempt to beach.
I knew that thirty years
Of getting up for work
Made you used to rising
In darkness which seemed to last
So long, it wouldn't let
Another day begin.
But we'd flown here to Australia
To spend a month: this
Was a vacation, the father-
And-son kind we two
Never took before.
I yawned that I'd pass—waking
Late was my way of telling
I didn't have to drive
My bus back in Seattle.
You're going to miss this light,
You said, but I lay still.
After three days, you stopped
Asking me to join you.
A decade has gone by
Since I drifted through the dark
While you walked out in dawns
Which made the jacaranda
Glow, the eucalyptus
Peel back its bark. You were right,
Father: I miss that light.

ROUNDABOUT

Our plan was not to have a plan: we'd fly
To Australia—for you, the land of World War II—
And see whatever came our way. The sky
Below the equator shimmered hot and blue,
As though we'd crossed the dateline into summer.
At Melbourne Airport, we rented a car,
Deciding I would drive, then walked around
To the wrong sides. You shook your head and grinned:
Looks like someone moved the steering wheel.
The driver by default, as you pulled out
You barely missed a shuttle van. Our hotel
Lay just a few miles off by map. We hit
The freeway right at rush hour, the lorries
Screaming by us. I felt the blasts of wind seize
Our car and shake it, as if the trucks frightened
The air away from them. At last we found
The exit into town. My eyes on the map,
I wasn't watching when the roundabout
Sucked us in. I thought of a whirlpool that traps
A small boat. *Which road will lead us out?*
You asked, dodging other drivers as we looped
And looped the tarmac ring. But the signs whipped
By too quick for me to read. Then the swirl
Of cars parted briefly; you zagged through a snarl
Of horns, finding the spoke that let us escape.
Afraid, I had you drive the first two days,
Asking how you kept it straight. *I keep
My body near the centerline—that way*

My turns will end up right. Now you've taken
An exit I can't see, while I go on
Circling the same place until the land
Spins, and the map crumples in my hands.

III. THE UNBROKEN CODE

NISQUALLY BAY

The boy, not knowing he's a Pisces, grips
The dry and splintered edge of the raft, kicking
Till he makes a froth of the glinting inlet.
His father's walking somewhere up the beach—
Skipping stones, he bets: his dad can keep
A pebble floating longer than anyone.
Uncle Bill, who owns this acre of water,
Asks his father to come fishing. But his dad
Says he's no good at catching things. The boy
Allows his legs to sink, dunking his head
While he holds the raft, his eyes sealed tight
As razor clams. When his stretching toes touch
The sand below, he bounces up, then sinks
Again, laughing when he surfaces,
As if not sure which world—wet or sun—
To stay in. His jumping makes the raft slide
Sideways. Not knowing there's a small channel,
The trail cut when the tide leaves the bay,
He's surprised when now he keeps on sinking
Like one of his father's stones reaching the end
Of its arc. His eyes pop open: water
Becomes his new sky, the cloud of his breath
Wobbling upward to the raft he can't grasp.
He feels something snag his wrist—he struggles
To wrench loose. Then he's hanging in the air,
Gasping and wet the same as the time he left
His first ocean. He squints in the sudden light
To see his father holding him up like a trophy.

THE PADDLE

When I was small, the only game I knew
That used a paddle was the one where you
Would tell me to line up with Dan and Jack—
Since I was oldest, I'd be first—then whack

Our tails with a thin fan of pale wood.
For cursing (that shortcut to adulthood)
Or fighting with each other, we'd wait for the squeal
Of brakes in the driveway. Mom would reveal

Our sins, and then—after correcting flaws
In blueprints all day—you'd enforce the laws
Of grown-ups. I even thought it might be fun
For you: you asked if we knew the things we'd done

Were wrong before you gave us "what we deserved,"
Although you never laughed, and your mouth curved
Down. Did you imagine, raising your hand,
You were batting the ball on the rubber band?

But when from rain or boredom we made some crack,
Committing the offense of talking back
To Mother (the worst charge she could level),
That paddle vanished, and *The Red Devil*—

Our name for the bigger one you hid in a drawer,
The one whose lacquer glared dark as the door
To hell—would burn our butts like a brand.
It took me growing up to understand

This wasn't a game. You knew your sons were vessels
Making passage across a sea of evils,
And showed us salt was what remained of tears.
With every stroke, you brought us closer to shore.

MY FATHER WASHING DISHES (I)

That summer in Seattle I was six.
In the sweaty night, though I could hardly keep
My eyes from closing toward sleep,

I wandered to the den to watch TV:
My father was so silent, and boys
Are always seeking noise.

But through the voice of the toy commercial,
I heard another sound: high
And wavery like the cry

Of a creature unused to singing. Aware at last
It wasn't coming from the screen,
I got up to lean

Around the kitchen corner—there stood my father
Slowly rubbing a fingertip
Along the rigid lip

Of a glass, drawing music from its mouth.
He glanced at me, gave a thin smile,
Then dried the glass with his towel.

MY FATHER WASHING DISHES (II)

I knew there was a wall between the den
And kitchen, and that Dad liked to joke
Even less than talk.

Rare as a snowball in summer, Mom would say;
His folks didn't raise him like that.
One August night as I sat

Before the TV—some show whose father laughed
And gave his son's back a slap—
Into my drowsy lap

Fell something white: a napkin wadded up
In a ball. I looked around; no one.
Dad was in the kitchen,

Washing the dinner dishes. Another paper
Meteor sailed down. Who
Was doing this, and how?

Scanning the wall between the kitchen and den,
I saw for the first time—at the top
Near the ceiling—a gap.

AN ENGINEERING PROBLEM

I'm not sure why my father built the rack
My brothers and I would use to stretch the limbs
Of the little doll my sister liked so much.

Called a "Sleepy Doll," it was more a puppet—
Its head about the size of a golf ball
Which smelled of sawdust, hands and feet

Rounded down to spheres, the limp body
Dressed in powder blue pajamas. Its eyes
Were always closed. Maybe we boys wanted

To open them: apprentice torturers,
We had to start on something small. Hanging
The doll by its neck from a string noose would make

Our sister, too short to reach it, cry.
Then, growing bored of that, we went to Dad.
We knew he loved his daughter—we used to whine

He never spanked her hard like us. I think
To him it was an engineering problem:
He cut and measured carefully, as though

His boss at Boeing had given him the job.
On the stock he nailed a brass hook, curved
As a scythe, to lock the doll's ankles in place.

For the roller with the twine to bind its wrists,
He built a handle like the one I'd seen
On an old clothes wringer at a junk store.

He even carved a wheel spiked with ratchets
To fix the handle to, so we could mimic
The creaks and clanks we heard from the real thing

In horror movies. The tighter we cranked, the more
Our sister shrieked: a strange ventriloquism.
But no machine I ever knew could make

My father talk. Instead of words, I remember
The way he sanded the rack smooth as talc—
The powder he rubbed us with when we would climb

Out of the tub, before we went to sleep.
As I hold the toy in my hand, I slide my fingers
Over its wood, feeling for a sliver.

THE BAYOU DRIVE-IN

A Mustang or Corvette—
The kind of car whose ad
Shows a girl lying flat
As a coat of paint on the hood—

I dreamed of getting one.
But all I heard was the mutter
Of the beat-up station wagon
My parents drove for years.

The two-toned Mercury
With the eroding green panels
Carried my friends and me
In everything but style.

Thirteen, forbidden to date,
I still knew that no "chick
With measurements" would sit
In such an uncool wreck.

I'm talking about the sort
Of girls in horror movies
Built like Hazel Court
With fire for hair, ice for eyes,

And breasts with a capital B
Bulging from her low-cut gown
Or caressed by her negligee
In *The Curse of Frankenstein*.

How often passion appears
A monstrous curse. The crevasse
Between girls like her
And me couldn't be crossed

By a station wagon.
So Dad would take us guys
To the Bayou Drive-In.
To keep the mosquitoes

Outside in the moist night,
He'd unwrap a small coil
Of bug repellent. When he lit
Its tip, I thought of candles

A priest would light for Mass.
Priests on the screen would burn
The monster with a cross
Or torch, and thereby warn

The townsfolk that Satan marks
The sinner. Hands together
While the sky went dark,
I'd lean as if in prayer

Or like a creature crouched
In wait for girls in nightgowns.
Soon Dad would sleep, slouched
By the steering wheel; the moon

Would cast its scarred glow
Over the gravel lot;
Our goddesses would grow
Limp in their lingerie and get

Carried off by villains
That never suffered guilt
Because they weren't human.
One night, saying we felt

So hot we'd like to die,
Me and Frank Sullivan
Begged Dad to let us lie
On the roof of the wagon.

Up there flat on our stomachs,
We laughed as loud as we dared
And swapped dirty jokes,
Searching for the right words.

Halfway through *The Horror
Of Dracula* (third
In the Triple Terror Feature),
I knew the noise I heard

Wasn't from the movie—
I looked down, staring
When I saw a girl and guy
Stretched out on the long

Bench-seat of a '55
Chevy one slot over.
I swallowed dryly, gave
Frank a nudge: a snore

His only answer. Alone
With their secret, I watched
As a different kind of groan
Which Hazel never matched

Began to take to the air.
Squinting, I could imagine
I really saw her bare
Breasts, flat like mine,

Their clothes rumpled and loose
As skin they wanted to shed.
They were going to a place
So far from me, it closed

Their eyes to open their throats.
How long would they go on?
I wondered, afraid I'd be caught.
With a grunt, the guy was done:

He lifted himself off.
The girl, rubbing her forehead,
Sat up slow and stiff
As one of the Undead

Bitten by the Vampire.
My heart thudding, I turned
Back to the screen, unsure
Of what I'd just learned.

Dad and Frank slept
Through the scary climax:
Dracula, trapped
Between a cross of candlesticks

And a shaft of blinding sun,
Was forced into the light.
He shrieked as it burned his skin
To ash; his last flight

Was on a scattering wind.
Waking Frank, I climbed back
To the ground. Her arm around
The guy's neck, she looked

At me, and then away.
Cars started to honk
As floodlights flared. The Chevy
Throomed like a beast, and Frank

Asked, *What did I miss?*
I couldn't tell him. Haunted
By her, I kept my face
Blank as stone: I wanted

To hold what I had seen.
When I got home, I found
The stains—dark and green—
That rubbed off on my hands.

THE UNBROKEN CODE

I.

The Plant demanded silence. Something thorned
And tangled as the blackberries which waved
Behind our house. Tentacles reaching
For me—this is what I saw when Mother
Said: *While Father's at the Plant, he's not allowed
To talk; he's building secret things.*

My comic books explained the Code of Silence—
I could see the ritual to get your job.
Tied to a chair as someone hissed questions,
You clamped your jaws tighter than the vise
Numbing your hand, and wouldn't even utter
Your name. You were the perfect man to draw

Blueprints of missiles and anti-missile
Missiles whose letters never spelled a word.
The rockets you designed flew astronauts
Two hundred fifty thousand miles away—
To a place beyond sound. For you, these heroes
Signed a giant photo of the moon.

II.

I thought for years all fathers held their tongues.
Your children nearly grown, the family ringed
The Christmas tree; to catch our banter, Mom
Set out a tape recorder. When it played back,
Your voice was missing: as if you weren't there.

Near middle age, I crossed the ocean with you
To Australia. We swam through water hiding
The Great Barrier Reef. Jellyfish trailed
Tentacles in the vast cold your sub had patrolled,
Where the slightest word could be your death.

I asked about torpedoes. Short as a fuse
Or the rapid taps of Morse you'd sent
As a radar man, you quoted your father—
Useless talk is so much crow-squawking.
I wondered why you'd been born with a mouth.

III.

Now you are gone. Attempting to construct
The puzzle of your past from these fragments,
A meager handful, I'm forced to cut my own.

I learned your father left his family nothing—
No money, food, or word when he'd return—
The times he'd disappear for weeks in the swamp

To hunt. His girlfriends were a secret, too;
One the whole town whispered. What promise
Made you keep those other secrets? Did you blame

Yourself for the way your mother died?
That day, Grandfather leaves once more to hunt
"Two-legged deer." Your mother sends you out

To play, then sets the house on fire. Lifting
His shotgun, she ends her darkness with a shout
Of light. You never spoke of this: thorns

Had wrapped your throat, cinching off the words.
I didn't see—your flesh sealed over the barbs.

CRUSH DEPTH

A man who went to war beneath the sea
Knew the weight of water. He knew dark
Pressing a submarine more closely
Than earth that surrounds a coffin could mark

The steel he wore for a shell. The burden shut
All sight, made each breath a betraying wind.
It separated his craft from a ship that cut
The surface—pinging, a churning hiss. Being found

Brought depth charges packed so full
Of sound, they were death. Shaken in the black,
His boat once had to go too deep. The hull
Buckled. Staring, he thought the skin would crack

As pressure pounded his ears. The sub had gone
Below crush depth but escaped the hunter.
This man knew the weight of water goes on
Squeezing something inside until it splinters.

FATHER GATHERS HIS BREATH

In the early dark,
I'd wake—those mornings, before you shaved
To leave for work, you'd come into my room
And kiss me goodbye. Moonlight
Washed the room the palest blue
As though it were underwater. Your whiskers felt
Like small needles;
Five years old, sometimes I'd lie still,
Pretending to be asleep.
You'd blow gently on my face, and wait
For my eyes to open.

The unseen light
Of X-rays found the spots of light growing
Quietly in your lungs. Your last year,
You went back to the Florida beach
Where you swam when young.
Your short, clipped strokes
Fought the water, not letting it touch
Your face. Home again, you hammered
The flight of stairs you'd put off fixing—
Each *whack!* like a gunshot—and sanded the rail
Smooth as you shaved.

You died at home in August,
A blue moon about to rise. When Mother called,
You lay on your couch, your breath rapid
Like a diver getting ready
To enter the sea. I think you hung on,
Waiting for me, so she wouldn't be alone.

Kneeling beside you, I called
Your name, but you had begun the arc.
I watched your eyes close. Your whiskers
Prickled my lips. I stopped myself
From blowing on your face.

ABOUT THE AUTHOR

Michael Spence spent a hitch as a naval officer aboard the aircraft carrier USS *John F. Kennedy* (CV-67), which is now decommissioned. For the last twenty-five years, he has driven public-transit buses in the Seattle area. He has had two previous collections published: *The Spine* (Purdue University Press, 1987) and *Adam Chooses* (Rose Alley Press, 1998). In 1990, Spence received a Creative Writing Fellowship from the National Endowment for the Arts. *Crush Depth* was twice a finalist for The New Criterion Poetry Prize. His work has also appeared in numerous journals.